A STEP-BY-STEP BOOK ABOUT
PARROTS

ELAINE RADFORD

Photography: Glen Scott Axelrod, Dr. Herbert R. Axelrod, T. Brosset, Tom Caravaglia, Rod Cathcart, Chelman and Petrulla, Michael Gilroy, Harry V. Lacey, P. Leysen, Irene and Michael Morcombe, Elaine Radford, San Diego Zoo, Harold Schultz, Vogelpark Walsrode.
Humorous drawings by Andrew Prendimano.

Distributed in the UNITED STATES by T.F.H. Publications, Inc., One T.F.H. Plaza, Neptune City, NJ 07753; in CANADA to the Pet Trade by H & L Pet Supplies Inc., 27 Kingston Crescent, Kitchener, Ontario N2B 2T6; Rolf C. Hagen Ltd., 3225 Sartelon Street, Montreal 382 Quebec; in CANADA to the Book Trade by Macmillan of Canada (A Division of Canada Publishing Corporation), 164 Commander Boulevard, Agincourt, Ontario M1S 3C7; in ENGLAND by T.F.H. Publications Limited, Cliveden House/Priors Way/Bray, Maidenhead, Berkshire SL6 2HP, England; in AUSTRALIA AND THE SOUTH PACIFIC by T.F.H. (Australia) Pty. Ltd., Box 149, Brookvale 2100 N.S.W., Australia; in NEW ZEALAND by Ross Haines & Son, Ltd., 18 Monmouth Street, Grey Lynn, Auckland 2, New Zealand; in SINGAPORE AND MALAYSIA by MPH Distributors (S) Pte., Ltd., 601 Sims Drive, #03/07/21, Singapore 1438; in the PHILIPPINES by Bio-Research, 5 Lippay Street, San Lorenzo Village, Makati Rizal; in SOUTH AFRICA by Multipet Pty. Ltd., 30 Turners Avenue, Durban 4001. Published by T.F.H. Publications, Inc. Manufactured in the United States of America by T.F.H. Publications, Inc.

Contents

INTRODUCTION

The hardy, intelligent birds known as parrots have charmed humans down through the ages. From Alexander the Great to King Henry VIII and beyond, people have always been fascinated by a feathered creature that could mimic human tongues. Today, parrots are more popular than ever before. Thanks to airplanes that can carry birds quickly from all corners of the globe and to breeders who specialize in raising these interesting birds, you can easily find a friendly parrot that fits your purse and your lifestyle.

Parrots make attractive avian pets for several reasons. Since they eat an omnivorous diet heavy in carbohydrates, they thrive on a seed-based menu that's convenient and inexpensive to feed. Because most of the popular varieties prefer to exercise by climbing rather than flying, they're happy in indoor cages as well as elaborate outdoor aviaries. And because they're highly intelligent, they can learn a range of tricks and interesting behaviors that keep the parrot owner entertained.

You have a world of choices when you're shopping for a parrot (or hookbill, as they're sometimes called). Want a good talker or cuddler? A small, quiet pal that's right for apartment living? A big, bold companion that can take a little rough and tumble? A clever trick bird? A gentle sweetheart? All these possibilities—and more—are yours when you enter the diverse and exciting world of parrots.

FACING PAGE:
An African Grey Parrot. African Greys are considered to be one of the most intelligent of all parrot species; they have the capacity to acquire a very large vocabulary.

Choosing Your Parrot

You could be overwhelmed by choices when you first start considering a parrot. Your options range from the petite Budgerigar (or Parakeet, as it's often called in the United States) to the magnificent Macaws. I don't promise that deciding on just one will be easy, but you can make sure that the parrot you choose is right for you by considering your lifestyle, your budget, and what you hope for from a hookbill pet.

If you're a first time bird owner looking for a playful pet that could learn to talk, you should give first consideration to two categories of parrots: young Budgerigars and Cockatiels or hand-reared parrots of any species. The rankest beginner can tame a Budgie or Cockatiel acquired before it reaches sexual maturity, often convincing the newcomer to sit on a finger or shoulder within minutes of beginning the first lesson. (However, if talking is really important to you, keep in mind that the chatty Budgerigar is much more likely to learn to talk than the Cockatiel.) Parrots hand-reared by human breeders go that one better: they don't have to be tamed at all! Because they consider the human hand-rearer their parent, they have a trusting, affectionate attitude toward humans that makes them ideal for beginners.

Hand-reared parrots are more expensive than imports or parent-bred birds because they require a lot of human labor and because they're in great demand. If you have your heart set on a particular species of parrot, you may have to get on a waiting list for a hand-fed pet. However, the wait should be well worth it. A hand-fed baby is more likely to talk, less likely to bite, and infinitely eager for human petting and pampering.

If you opt for an untame parrot, be sure to get a young bird. Taming adult parrots, even small ones like Lovebirds and Budgies, is for experts. If you haven't spent much time looking at birds before, you may need a little help determining a parrot's age by sight. Keep in mind that most young parrots have slimmer bodies, shorter tails, and duller colors than the adults, since it's more important for a youngster to stay hidden from predators than to attract a mate.

Many groups of parrots also sport their own special marks of youth. Very young Lovebirds, for instance, have black

on their beaks. Young Budgerigars display bars on their forehead that recede as they grow up. Immature Senegal Parrots have brownish rather than grey heads. Young African Grey Parrots have grey eyes, while adults have yellow eyes. Sun Conures start out with green backs that gradually change to the beautiful yellow. Once you're looking seriously at a particular bird, you can check the chapter on the parrot groups for more hints on distinguishing the youngsters from the adults. And don't hesitate to consult other books or other bird owners—and feel free to ask the seller lots of questions.

If you have a choice between a small untame parrot and a large one, most beginners will do best with the smaller bird. Although larger parrots can be more intelligent and hence

A lovely Scarlet Macaw. Note the rainbow of colors on its wings. All Macaws species have long pointed tails and a bare area on the face.

A trio of Budgerigars. Budgies come in a wide variety of colors, and they offer something for everyone.

easier to train in the long run, they can inflict some painful bites—and people who are too intimidated by their birds to train them properly are doomed to disappointment. Yes, you can always send the bird to a trainer if you find you can't tame it, but 1) good parrot trainers are hard to find, and 2) the sooner the bird is tamed, the more affectionate and trustworthy

it will become. The smaller parrots can be as exotic and beautiful as the larger ones, and they are often less expensive. There's certainly no harm in looking over the Conures, the Ringneck Parakeets, or the Quaker Parakeets before you make up your mind.

Before you reach a final decision on your parrot, you should also consider your lifestyle. Many parrots, especially the hand-reared ones, expect a lot of time and attention. If you work at home or enjoy sharing your TV hours with your feathered friend, you should do fine even if you do take the occasional vacation or overnight business trip. However, if you're so busy that you can play with your parrot only for a few minutes each night or on the weekend, you may want to reconsider your choice. That affectionate baby could turn into a demanding screamer if you can't give it the attention it needs. You might be better off purchasing two small parrots that can entertain each other; a pair of Budgerigars, Lovebirds, or Cockatiels is a good choice. True, the members of the pair will never approach the tameness of a single pet, but they will be happy to amuse you with their antics rather than driving you nuts with their screeching. If you really prefer a tame single pet, you may want to consider the independent Amazons; unlike many other parrots, these self-sufficient birds seem content to spend a large part of each day alone as long as they have enough room and toys to keep themselves entertained.

Do all you can to ensure that your new parrot is a legal bird in top condition. Unfortunately, many unscrupulous individuals prey on beginners and bargain-hunters by smuggling in parrots from Mexico and other countries where their export is prohibited. These smuggled birds are often traumatized by their trip across the border in small, uncomfortable containers and their subsequent treatment by people who care more about profit than birds. As a result, they may carry contagious or stress-related diseases. Some may even belong to rare or endangered species. And, of course, buying smuggled goods is itself a crime.

To avoid getting mixed up in a situation that will lead to nothing but heartache, investigate your sellers very carefully. Parrots imported legally into the United States are banded at

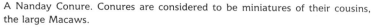

the quarantine station, so if a wild-caught bird lacks a band, you should ask why. Never buy a bird at a flea market, from the back of a truck, or at a price that's much lower than what you'd pay elsewhere for a comparable bird. In the long run, that bargain will prove much too expensive.

You can buy with confidence from a pet shop or a breeder if you inform yourself about what to expect before you buy. (Smugglers rely on ignorance and the universal desire to save a buck.) Read over the chapter on breeding and understand what's involved in producing healthy parrots before you shop. Once you see what's involved in breeding, say, Amazon Parrots, you'll see why it's highly unlikely that someone would be able to breed them consistently for bargain basement prices.

A shop or breeder can be large or small. What's really important is the seller's care and cleanliness. Are the perches,

A Nanday Conure. Conures are considered to be miniatures of their cousins, the large Macaws.

A pair of White-headed Pionus Parrots. Healthy parrots should be alert and aware of their surroundings.

cups, and drinkers reasonably clean? Does the bottom of the cage look like it was cleaned within the last 24 hours? Is there a place for the large, tame parrots to play so that they won't lose their lively spirits and fondness for humans while awaiting sale? Are the birds and cages scent-free? Except for some Amazons, healthy parrots shouldn't have an odor.

If the shop looks good, you're ready to inspect the individual that interests you. Is the parrot reasonably alert? Although parrots siesta in the middle of the day, a healthy one won't be so deeply asleep that it doesn't know you're there. Expect it to open an eye and regard you with interest (if it's somewhat tame) or alarm (if it isn't). A hand-reared parrot may actively solicit your attention by saying, "Hello," or by bowing its head to solicit a scratching. Great!

Beginners should be fairly picky about their new parrot's plumage. It's true that perfectly healthy parrots must molt and many playful youngsters have ragged tails. However, a newcomer to parrots isn't ready to figure out which bald spots are harmless defects that will soon grow out and which are the

result of disease or self-inflicted injury. You should also check the eyes, nostrils, and vent; if there is matting or discharge at any of these body openings, the bird is probably sick and should be rejected. The bird must also be plump enough to withstand a few hours or even a day of sulking, so feel its keel bone (the one running the length of its breast) to make sure it's well padded by flesh.

I strongly advise against beginners attempting rescue missions. Buying a weak parrot kept under poor conditions usually does more harm than good. You're not only encouraging the seller to continue with slipshod practices, you may be presenting the parrot with more change than it's ready to handle now. Although it's an exaggeration that parrots are content to spend their lives on one tree, they do tend to take a few days to get accustomed to new quarters and new people. A sick bird most definitely isn't up to the stress of adapting to anything new.

Ask about the seller's return policy. Many sellers will allow you to return the bird if a vet finds something wrong with it within a reasonable amount of time. For your protection, it's best to get your guarantee in writing.

Finally, ask the seller to clip the wings of an untame parrot. By the time the feathers grow back, the parrot should be tame enough to let you do this chore yourself. For now, however, it's best to let the seller do it so that the bird associates any power struggle involved with the seller and not with you. I strongly advise against attempting to tame an unclipped parrot because the frightened bird could get away from you and fly into a wall so hard it breaks its neck. Wing-clipping is painless and far more dignified than a concussion, so don't let misplaced sympathy put a parrot's life in danger.

By the way, don't let standard precautions stand in the way of owning a parrot. Although any animal can get sick or have an accident, parrots are remarkably long-lived birds. Even the smaller parrots can outlive a cat or dog, and the large parrots can live fifty or sixty years or even more. Make sure that you have room in your life for a long-term feathered friend before you go shopping for a parrot.

A lovely Turquoisine Parrot. Before purchasing any type of parrot, be sure to check it thoroughly. An unhealthy bird is no bargain.

HOUSING

Most parrots do well in human homes because they enjoy exercising by climbing rather than flying and, hence, accept reasonably small cages.

If your pet parrot spends most of the day outside of the cage, it will need a smaller cage than a pair of birds or an individual that must spend most of its day confined. However, all parrots must have a cage big enough to allow them to spread their wings and turn around without brushing the sides of the cage. Otherwise, they will feel cramped and their feathers will become frayed.

If you're away most of the day, be sure to give your parrot more generous accommodations. The cage should have room for a swing and one other toy, and it should permit the bird to climb up and down for some distance. You should have no trouble meeting these qualifications for a bird the size of a Conure, but you may have to special-order the proper cage for a Macaw or a Cockatoo. Obviously, you'll have to make do with something smaller in the interim, but you shouldn't get careless and put off getting the larger cage if you want your bird to stay at its most beautiful and content.

If you have a pair of small birds like Lovebirds or Cockatiels, do give them more room than the seller suggests for a single bird. Remember, it's easier for a cage to be too small than too large! Even the gentle Cockatiels or affectionate Lovebirds can get grouchy if they can never get more than an inch away from their companion. It's wisest to allow enough room for the birds to play apart as well as together. Can both birds climb up and down the walls of the cage at the same time? Is there room to include two toys without constantly bonking one

FACING PAGE:
A beautiful Red Lory. When selecting natural wood perches for your parrot, be sure that the wood has not been sprayed with chemicals for several years, as these sprays can be highly toxic to parrots.

14

bird on the beak? Can you attach a roost box to the side of the cage? If so, your small parrot pair should do just fine. Few beginners purchase a pair of large parrots, but if you do, you will need a large flight cage or an aviary—something we'll discuss in more detail in the chapter on breeding.

Remember that parrots are often called hookbills. When you combine powerful beaks and inquisitive minds, you get a parrot that can outwit a weak cage. I recommend that you give all parrots metal cages, even the smaller ones. At the very least, make sure that your smaller parrot can't reach any plastic or wooden parts. With the powerful Macaws, Amazons, African Greys, and other large parrots, you're just asking for trouble if you settle for less than an all-metal cage. Some of these wizards can even figure out how to open their own doors, so you may want to consider something that can be secured with a combination lock. An Amazon left to its own devices all day can be incredibly resourceful—and unbelievably destructive!

You can make your own cage, if you prefer, as long as you take into account the strength and determination of your parrot. Use strong welded wire, making sure that there are no

A pair of Black-headed Caiques. When setting up a cage for any type of Caique, be sure to provide a roost box into which they can burrow.

A lovely lutino mutation of the Indian Ringneck Parakeet in an outdoor aviary.

rough edges or wooden frame parts where the parrot can chew. Choose a door thoughtfully, and make sure it can be locked from the outside. It takes some work and care, but a home-made cage does have its advantages. Because it's substantially cheaper for its size, making your own could permit you to give your parrot a roomier, more comfortable cage than you could have purchased.

Some of the smaller cages meant for Lovebirds or Budgies contain plastic perches. Throw them away and replace them with wood. It's true that wood perches aren't immortal because parrots exercise their beak and nails on them so much, but that's actually all to the good. The more your parrot chews, the less likely you are to end up needing to trim its beak. And while the occasional toenail trimming is unavoidable, wood perches help keep the nails in better condition than plastic ones do.

Your parrot will be most comfortable on wood perches large enough to let it wrap its toes one-half to three-quarters of the way around. To prevent sore feet caused by putting pressure on the same spot all the time, use slightly different perches around the cage and on the parrot's playpen or T-stand. Natural perches are best of all. Sturdy natural birch branches are often offered in bird specialty shops for the larger parrots like the Macaws. You can supply the smaller parrots with green branches from apple, willow, or birch trees as long as you know that the trees haven't been sprayed with insecticide for several years.

A moment ago, I mentioned the parrot's playpen or T-stand. Every tame parrot should have one! By placing a stand or playpen in an area where you spend a lot of time, you can enjoy your pet's companionship while you talk with visitors, putter around the house, or just watch TV. In fact, I recommend that you buy or build a portable T-stand for smaller parrots so they can travel with you around the house. Although sometimes it may seem as if your parrot doesn't do much on the stand that it couldn't do in its cage, it really appreciates the freedom and companionship made possible by the playpen.

A pair of Scarlet-chested Parakeets. This species is still on the endangered list, although it has been bred in captivity and although its outlook has become brighter.

A Dusky Parrot (*Pionus fuscus*), a member of the Pionus Parrot group.

Let's face it, you're much more likely to talk to your parrot or offer it a head-scratching if it's sitting out on a stand rather than in a cage. More elaborate stands that include ladders and climbing bars are also highly recommended because they encourage otherwise lazy parrots to exercise. Change the ladders and toys around occasionally, and watch the parrot go exploring.

If a tame, trustworthy parrot has a stand and a play-pen, why does it need a cage? Here are two good reasons: your furniture and your bird's health. You should never leave an uncaged parrot unsupervised for more than a few seconds. Parrots, like toddlers, seem to learn about their world by putting it in their mouths. It just doesn't take very long for a powerful hookbill to bite into an electrical cord or put some interesting marks on a table leg. For your peace of mind, have a cage to put your parrot in when you go out or leave the room. Some people may prefer to use a leg chain to attach a larger parrot to its stand, but I just don't think that's wise. What if the parrot startled or tried to leap onto the floor while you were gone and got tangled in the chain? The disaster could be all over by the time you got home to help.

Where to put the cage? Just in case the parrot is nursing a secret illness, keep it away from all other pet birds for a full thirty days. After that, you can place the cage anywhere that's free of drafts, smoke, and strong odors. The kitchen is out, since the changing temperatures and cooking smells can overwhelm a bird's respiratory system. Once the parrot is tame, the family room or den is usually a great place for these curious birds because they can see what's going on and let you know when they want attention. A shy, untame parrot, however, may need to be placed in a more quiet spot until it's used to people and ready to interact with the family.

Cage covers are usually considered optional for quiet parrots, especially since parrots have such a good time chewing them into ratty holes. However, most parrots aren't always quiet, and you'll probably need a cover to let them know they're squawking too much. (Most birds won't make any noise when they're in total darkness.) You can also use a cover to let the bird know that it's time to settle down and get ready for sleep. Finally, a cage cover is a great way to tell all but the most forward late-night guests that the parrot needs its rest!

Other cage or playpen accessories include toys, nest boxes, and "bird protectors." The latter is a protective disk available in all pet stores that prevents mites from taking up residence in your bird's feathers. They should be hung outside the bird's cage and replaced at recommended intervals. Unfortunately, some of the medium-sized to larger parrots may think that chewing on the disk is great sport. It isn't. Try to place the disk in a location that the parrot can't reach. If that isn't possible, you may have to do without the protector. Fortunately, single pet parrots rarely acquire mites unless they have some access to the outdoors.

However, if your parrot is scratching furiously, it may be one of the unlucky ones. To find out for sure, place a white cover over the bird's cage at night and check it early the next morning. If red mites are present, they will be shockingly obvious against the white cloth! Thoroughly clean the bird, its cage, any roost boxes, playpens, or toys, and consult your vet for additional help.

Of course, your bird could be scratching because it needs a bath. Most parrots enjoy being sprayed with a mister, while some smaller parrots prefer to wash themselves in a bird bath. After awhile, it will become obvious which technique your bird likes best.

For maximum safety, don't give plastic bird toys to any parrot other than a Budgie. The others are just too strong, and they could break the plastic and harm themselves. Good parrot toys have solid metal construction and sturdy wood, rawhide, or hard rubber parts. The best commercial toys for parrots are designed by people who know the beak of the parrot, so look for them in pet supply stores and bird specialty shops. For variety, supply your own cheap or free toys to the parrot. Most really enjoy destroying a broken or old-fashioned wooden clothespin (with no metal spring, of course), an old toilet paper roll, or even those magazine subscription post cards. Just make sure the proposed toy doesn't have any sharp edges or potentially breakable parts that could hurt a pet that doesn't know its own strength.

A pair of Hyacinth Macaws. Hyacinths are the largest parrots in the world.

Most single pet parrots don't require a roost box, but Lovebirds really appreciate a Budgie-sized one. If you have a pair of birds, there's no harm in offering them a roost box once they're sexually mature. Who knows? It could go from sleeping area to baby nest.

It's easy to keep your parrot cage clean—although the floor around it can often be another matter! Change the paper on the floor every day when you change the food and water drinkers, then vacuum or sweep up any feathers or seed husks around the cage. If you use corncob or other natural material to absorb odors and catch droppings, you can go a few days before changing the bottom if you stir the absorbent bedding daily. Once a week, wipe down all the bars and surfaces of the cage and T-stand. Don't forget to wipe down perches and toys! The droppings will wipe off metal surfaces very easily. However, to keep the perch and other wooden surfaces clean, you will probably have to use sandpaper or a perch scraper (a small stiff brush available in pet shops). Make a habit of cleaning as you go, and keeping these naturally neat birds clean should pose no problem.

Bourke Parakeet. Cleanliness is imperative in the parrot's environment.

A White Cockatoo. Cockatoos are amiable birds which when tamed require all the attention their owners can give them.

CARE AND FEEDING

Feeding a parrot a healthy diet doesn't require a Ph.D. in nutrition—really! Although people used to feeding a dog or a cat may initially think a parrot's demands are complicated, they really aren't hard to feed well if you yourself eat a nutritious diet. In the wild, parrots forage for all kinds of vegetable matter, especially seeding grasses and fruit, incidentally ingesting some animal matter like small insects. Therefore, they're much like people in that they require a varied diet to meet all of their nutritional needs.

In the past, people often expected their parrots to make do on seed, water, maybe some dried greens, and the occasional apple core. Then they scratched their heads and wondered why a spoiled pet whose favorite sport was snitching from human dinner plates outlived the rest of the birds. Fortunately, the growing interest in parrots has stimulated research into their nutrition, and today we know a lot more about what it takes to keep a parrot in peak condition.

There are three major components of nutritious food—carbohydrate, fat, and protein. The first two are the energy foods, and they've never been much of a problem. Carbohydrates are quick energy foods that are easily digested by the body for immediate use. Fats are complex, compact forms of energy that can be stored on the body for times of hardship or illness, and they're also an important ingredient in maintaining the health of a bird's feathers. Carbohydrates are readily available in seeds, vegetables, and fruits, while fats are present in many seeds, some nuts, and (of course) in the animal fats found in meat or eggs.

FACING PAGE:
An adorable Peach-front Conure. Conures and Macaws are prone to deficiencies in vitamin K; therefore, it is imperative to pay close attention to their diet.

Clearly, a bird on a seed diet won't have any trouble getting enough carbohydrate. And, if it's underweight or in poor feather, it isn't much harder to get more fat into its system: smaller parrots enjoy the oily seeds marketed as conditioning foods, while large parrots go for the calorie-rich sunflower seed.

The traditional diet, however, is much too low in protein for most parrots. Protein is the building material of the body, required for growing new cells and repairing sick or injured ones. Without protein, a young bird can't grow and an older bird can't fight disease or heal after an accident. Although parrots from arid grasslands like Budgerigars, Cockatiels, or Lovebirds are experts at extracting protein from relatively impoverished sources, any parrot will be healthier and more resistant to disease if it eats a good protein food.

In addition to the major forms of food, parrots (and all animals) also need the microscopic substances known as vitamins and minerals. Vitamins are complex compounds that help the body maintain health and repair damaged tissue efficiently, while minerals are simple elements used in the body's growth or maintenance. A deficiency in one key vitamin or mineral can set the stage for disease, sterility, or death. Although birds' bodies produce some of the B vitamins and vitamin C, pet parrots fed a traditional diet often lack sufficient vitamin A, vitamin D, and the mineral calcium. Since a bird needs these nutrients to keep its skeleton and respiratory system strong, you can see that allowing a deficiency of any one of these three is like setting a bomb that could go off at any time. Adult females are at especially high risk, since they may not be able to pass their eggs properly if they lack A, D, and calcium in proper proportions.

OK, so how do you go about making sure your parrot's diet contains everything it needs? There are several ways, so you are free to choose the method that best fits your own habits and budget—as well as the parrot's taste buds.

The easiest method involves the addition of a few simple-to-give, easy-to-find ingredients to the traditional seed-based diet. Parrots can eat any of several high protein foods, including mynah pellets, game bird pellets, or dog food. Large

An African Grey Parrot gnawing on a tree branch. Most parrots are active chewers; therefore, it is imperative that they are provided with perches and toys on which they can frequently gnaw.

parrots like Macaws will eat high-protein monkey biscuits like they're candy bars, so you can offer them one or two during the day. If your parrot is a good eater who feasts from both bowls, you can keep both the protein food and the seed in front of the bird at all times, allowing the bird to eat from each cup as it pleases. However, if it's a picky eater, you may have to coax it into eating the protein food by taking the seed away for a few hours a day. Few, like two or three, is the operative word here. Don't risk starving the bird. If it doesn't get curious enough to sample one kind of protein food after seeing it in its cup for several weeks in succession, try another kind.

You should also regularly test your seed to make sure it's fresh, since stale seed is low in vitamins. To make the test, get a sprouter from the health food store and follow the directions with some sample seeds from the parrot mix. If most of the seeds sprout in a few days, great! Give them to the parrot. Sprouts rate even higher in vitamins than the original seed. If

A Red Lory eating a piece of orange. Citrus fruits provide parrots with nutritious vitamins and minerals. Be sure, however, not to give your pet too much fruit.

few or none of the seeds sprout, it's time to toss the old mix and buy some new.

In addition to sprouts, you should offer your parrot a choice of other fresh vegetables and fruit on a daily basis. In fact, it's best to sprinkle vitamin powder on fresh food, since most of the powder sprinkled on seeds usually gets thrown away with the hull. With the exception of avocado, which may irritate some birds, you can offer your parrot any nutritious fruit or vegetable that you yourself could eat. However, make sure that the greens you give are really green. The pale iceberg lettuce that dominates American salads is almost totally devoid of any nutrient except water.

Don't be concerned if your parrot's droppings are somewhat looser after it has eaten a fresh fruit or vegetable. It's perfectly natural, not a symptom of illness as people mistakenly thought in the past. What can make your parrot ill is eating fruits and vegetables that are less than fresh. Remove any uneaten fresh food after 12 hours, sooner if the weather's really hot.

Another way to give your parrot a balanced diet is to base its menu on one of the new pelleted diets. Pellets, like seeds, are dry foods that can be left out overnight or while you're away for the weekend without permitting the growth of dangerous bacteria. (However, if your parrot soaks its pellets in water as many do, you should change the water and pellets every 12 hours.) The pellets also have the advantage of being scientifically formulated for exotic parrots, unlike dog food, monkey biscuits, or mynah pellets, which were obviously originally intended for other animals. People also like pellets because the mischievous parrot doesn't get any hulls to throw on the floor around the cage.

Most parrots, however, don't know that pellets are food at first, so you must switch them over from a seed diet slowly by mixing the pellets with the seed or by offering the pellets alone for a few hours a day. If the bird eats both, you may do well to permit it to continue on a mixed diet for the variety. I also feel that the parrot should continue to have access to some fresh fruits and vegetables, if only as a treat.

A third way to form the core of your parrot's diet is to mix a smorgasbord of cooked beans, fruits, and vegetables. If

A Turquoisine Parrot. In the wild, parrots are able to find their own balanced diet. It is the role of the owner of captive birds to provide his pets with the proper nutrition.

you're a vegetarian, you already know that eating beans with a grain vegetable like corn gives the body a complete protein. However, you really have to be a vegetarian or have a lot of birds to make this method practical, since you would have a lot of waste if you tried to make a sufficiently varied diet for a single parrot. I suggest consulting more advanced books or articles on parrot nutrition if you want to go the all-natural route.

In addition to the core food, the parrot should have access to clean water, a mineral block or cuttlebone, and a grit cup. If you wouldn't drink your tap water, don't give it to your birds, either. Let them share your spring or distilled water from a safe source. If you can use your tap water, boil it first to remove any chlorine that might cause problems for the bird. You can boil enough for several days at a time and store it in a bottle for future use.

The mineral block or cuttlebone helps ensure that your parrot gets enough calcium and other minerals. It can be left in the cage until eaten or soiled. Although it may seem as if your parrot goes for weeks without touching the mineral block, always keep it available. You never know when your parrot will feel a sudden need for calcium and proceed to devour the block with a speed which will amaze you.

Grit should be placed in a small cup of its own and left out until soiled. Your parrot shouldn't eat much grit, but it will occasionally take a little to aid its digestion. (Since they don't have teeth, birds swallow small bits of grit to help them grind up their food.) However, a sick or stressed parrot will sometimes gorge on grit, perhaps in the mistaken belief that it will help. To prevent this problem, always remove the grit cup when the bird is upset about something (like a new cage location or your recent vacation) or when it's feeling under the weather.

Some kinds of parrots have special requirements that you need to be aware of. Budgies, for instance, often lack iodine, so you may want to add an iodine-enriched supplement to a Budgie's diet if it never touches its cuttlebone or mineral block. Conures and mini Macaws tend toward a deficiency of vitamin K, so you need to encourage them to eat K-rich foods like turnip greens, broccoli, spinach, and deep green lettuces.

Care and Feeding

African Greys seem to need more calcium than other parrots, so you should sprinkle their fruit treats with calcium powder scraped from the cuttlebone and encourage them to sample high-calcium snacks like cheese. We're learning more about avian dietary requirements all the time, so you should read a bird-oriented publication regularly to keep up on new discoveries that can help you feed your birds better.

A few parrots do have rather specialized diets. Beginners may encounter the Brush-tongued Parrots, the Lories and Lorikeets, which are adapted to eat pollen, nectar, and fruit. You can make or buy a sugar-water nectar to feed these birds, but this substance provides only calories and isn't enough for a complete diet. The real core of the Lories' diet is a variety of fresh fruits, including apples, oranges, bananas, and grapes sprinkled with an avian vitamin-mineral powder. You should also offer them regular access to pellets, mealworms, and even minced lean meat. They may not accept these nutritious foods at first, but you should continue to try high-protein foods so that they'll be available when the bird feels a need for them.

Many parrots will enjoy sharing meals with you. To keep a feathered head out of your plate, offer the parrot its

A pair of young blue Scarlet-chested Parakeets. If you plan to keep a number of parrots together, be sure all the birds receive sufficient amounts of food.

own bowl of nutritious people food. Such treatment isn't spoiling if you feed yourself right. Parrots actually benefit from a taste of lean meat, cheese, whole grain bread or pasta, lightly cooked vegetables, and salads tossed with a minimum of dressing. Larger parrots like Amazons and Macaws even enjoy chewing on a chicken bone with a little meat left on it.

Of course, junk food that's bad for you is also bad for your parrot. Avoid eating cakes, candy bars, ice creams, cookies, and the like around your parrot. Sure, there's no harm in giving the parrot a treat if you only have a candy bar on Christmas. But if you eat sugary desserts every week, you're just asking for trouble if you share with the parrot. It's far better to distract the bird with its own fun food, such as the specially formulated treat bells or a bundle of spray millet.

Regular baths and a healthy diet go a long way toward bringing a parrot into top condition. However, you may need to perform a few other chores to keep your parrot at its best.

If you want to take your parrot outside or to public places, you must keep its wings well-clipped. Even a beautifully tame bird can be startled, and you would be heartbroken if a frightened pet flew away only to get lost and never find its way home again. If you keep your parrot at home, you must decide for yourself whether or not to clip those wings. If you're at all absent-minded about open windows or doors, or if your bird frequently startles, do keep those wings clipped to prevent an accident or escape.

If you have a large parrot, take it to a pet groomer's or pet shop for the first few times so that you can watch an expert trim its wings. If you have a smaller bird and a partner, you can probably do the job from the beginning at home. A hand-reared baby may sit placidly while you spread the wings and trim the long feathers at the end of the wing. Be sure, however, to learn the proper way from a professional before any cutting is done.

However, if your bird won't let you spread its wing, you can wrap it gently in a towel and have a partner hold it while you trim. Remember, never press against a bird's abdomen while holding it, or you could cut off its breathing.

Sometimes a parrot's beak and nails become overgrown. Beginners should let an expert like a vet or a pet

A blue mutation of the Indian Ringneck Parakeet. Birds, like people, have individual preferences when it comes to food. Get to know your pet and its likes and dislikes.

groomer take care of the beak, but you can trim a smaller parrot's nails without much difficulty, once you've learned the proper method from a professional, and once the bird is tame. Again, if the bird won't stand still for a nail-clipping, wrap it in a towel and let a partner hold it firmly but gently while you clip off the very end of the nail. If the parrot has light nails, you'll be able to see the dark vein running through them. Always cut below that vein. If the parrot has dark nails, you won't be able to see the vein, so cut very carefully and take only a little off each end in any one session.

Just in case, always have some styptic powder and a damp towel handy when trimming wings or toenails. If you accidentally cut into a blood feather or the vein in the bird's toe, quickly dab some of the powder on the towel and hold it firmly against the bleeding area. After a few seconds, the bleeding should stop.

TAMING, TRAINING

If your parrot was hand-reared, it should already be tame. Otherwise, you'll want to start working with your bird as soon as possible. Give it a day or two to get used to its new surroundings, make sure it's eating, and then get ready for lesson one. Please don't put it off. The earlier you start taming your parrot, the more affectionate and responsive it will be in the long run.

To tame a parrot, you need a bird-safe area that's free from distractions, some special treats like grape halves or sunflower seeds, and a stick sturdy enough to hold the parrot's weight. Prepare the taming room by removing breakables, covering mirrors and windows, and turning off any radios or TVs. If your bathtub can be shut off from the rest of the room with a door, you may find that the tub is just the place. (However, be sure to put down the toilet seat and cover the mirrors in case the bird does somehow escape.) Wherever you set up the training area, lock all doors and windows from the inside and request the rest of the family to stay away for awhile. It's less confusing for the bird if only one person at a time tries to do the training.

Don't use gloves to train a bird. Many parrots, especially imported ones, associate gloves with the traumatic experience of being captured and held by a stranger. Some parrots are so terrified of gloves that you won't be able to train them as long as the gloves are present; others will simply be a little cooler toward you than they might have been otherwise. Choose a parrot that you feel comfortable working with, and be prepared to move slowly in order to prevent accidents.

FACING PAGE:
A lovely Senegal Parrot. Before beginning your
pet's training, set aside a prepared area which
has been parrot-proofed.

Shiny objects, on the other hand, present an irresistible lure to parrots, so don't wear a watch or any jewelry during training or any time you're handling a parrot. I know from experience that a small parrot's beak is perfectly capable of turning a watch knob until it breaks.

Start the taming by opening the door of the bird's cage. Talk to it all the while, telling it how pretty it is and how much you want to make friends. Don't be concerned if it seems nervous at first. Give it time to see that you don't intend to stick your hand in and grab it. With luck, the parrot may get curious and climb out on its own. If so, praise it to the skies and move your hand toward it very slowly to offer it the treat.

More timid birds may not make any move to leave the cage. If it's a Cockatiel or Budgerigar, move your treat-holding hand toward the cage slowly, talking to it all the while. If it hisses or pulls back in fright, stop moving your hand for a few minutes, but don't pull back. Let the parrot see that having your hand nearby is no threat. After a time, you can get close enough to offer the bird the treat through the cage bars.

If your parrot isn't a Budgie or a Cockatiel, don't try to stick your fingers in the cage. Most parrots regard such intrusion as an invasion of their territory—even after they're tame. Instead, slowly move the perch into the cage, stopping for a minute or two each time the bird shows alarm. Again, never pull back. You don't want to teach the parrot that a good screech will make you disappear, do you?

Whether the bird is on top of or inside of its cage, move the perch toward it slowly, from the side. (Birds don't like a head-on approach because it resembles the behavior of a predator.) Place the perch lengthwise against the bird's chest. At this point, the parrot is sure to give in to its instinct to step up, since standing a little taller makes it feel in better control of the situation. If it doesn't step up, you're probably not holding the perch high enough. Again, once it takes a step, praise it in a soft but pleased tone.

If the bird bites you or steps on your head at any point, say "No" in a loud voice and use the perch to move it back where you want it. Never hit or punish a bird in any way, since they learn nothing from punishment but fear.

How far you go in the first lesson depends upon the bird. For best results, spend only 20 minutes at a time taming the bird. When the time is up, let it rest for at least an hour before beginning anew. Of course, it's better to end each session on a high note than to simply quit when a timer goes off. If the bird is sitting on your perch at the end of 15 minutes, go ahead and offer it a treat, praise it highly and put it back in its cage for a rest.

After a few lessons, it will become noticeably easier to get the parrot to step on the stick or to accept a treat from your fingers. At that point, you can teach it to step onto your finger or your arm, depending upon the size of the bird. You can often get it to step onto your arm by holding the perch down low, so that the parrot must climb up onto your arm to get up high. (Wear an old shirt with sleeves, so its claws will have something

A pair of Amazon Parrots. Amazon Parrots are extremely intelligent birds, and they have quite a long lifespan.

to grab.) With a small bird, you can simply hold the perch in one hand while approaching the bird slowly with the other. Hold your finger up to its chest, and it will soon step up. All the while, keep talking and praising the bird. Don't jerk back your hand when the parrot uses its beak to steady itself on its unfamiliar perch. It rarely means to bite, at least at first. Of course, if you tease the parrot by repeatedly jerking back your hand, it may well get irritated with you.

Parrots learn at different rates, of course. You may have a Budgie sitting on your hand at the end of the first 15 minute lesson. Or, it may take a good week for you to convince an African Grey to stop growling when you insert a stick into its cage. Even within a species, some individuals will be more confident than others. Be patient, and don't give up.

After a week or so, you will notice your parrot actually looking forward to the taming sessions. Why shouldn't it? It's getting treats and praise, things most parrots enjoy immensely. At this point, when the parrot is squawking to tell you to "come here" rather than to "go away," the bird is technically tame. However, I recommend taking a few extra lessons to teach the parrot to let you scratch its head and place your hand over its body. You'll be glad you did the first time you must trim the bird's nails or hold it for a vet exam.

Go slow, keep talking, and always remember to move your hand in from the side so that the parrot can see it coming. A good time to make your move might be when the parrot already has a treat in its beak that it would be reluctant to drop. In any case, carefully begin to scratch around the bird's ears and crown. Not too hard! After a moment, many parrots will fluff up their head feathers and shut their eyes in pure pleasure—a sure sign the bird trusts you and enjoys what you're doing.

After a few head-scratching sessions, you can begin slowly moving your hands over the bird's back. If it's a smaller bird, you can work up to holding it around its wings with one hand. With a larger bird, take more time and work on convincing it to accept both hands being held gently around its body. After a time, a Cockatoo or Macaw may be tickled pink by your petting. To be honest, though, most parrots will never be that

thrilled about having your hands around their body. As long as they can accept it quietly, however, you have done what you can to make sure they can be groomed or given a veterinary exam with minimal stress.

Now that your parrot is a tame member of the family, you can begin to train it to talk or do tricks. Again, the earlier you get to work, the better. Old parrots can learn new tricks, but they may not care to if you haven't established a pattern of teaching them games or words in the past. African Greys often

A pied Bourke Parrot. Wooden dowels are an essential item for the taming and training process.

require several months or even a year of lessons before they startle you with some surprisingly clear speech, but most parrots won't ever talk if they haven't started trying in the first few months in the household.

Individuals from just about every commonly kept parrot species have learned to talk. However, members of some parrot species are more likely to talk than others. African Greys and the various Amazon Parrots usually talk well, with surprisingly clear voices, if they're taught with patience from an early

age. The chatty little Budgerigars can learn to say all kinds of things, but their voices tend to remain fairly scratchy. Cockatoos and Macaws can have fine, clear voices, but they often stop with just a few words. If you know what to expect from your parrot, you can avoid disappointment—and, if you do succeed in convincing a fairly quiet bird like a Cockatiel to talk, you will also know what an accomplishment you've performed.

Use a combination of personal and electronically assisted teaching. There is no substitute for placing the tame parrot on your arm or finger and repeating the word you want it to learn over and over in a clear voice. However, one human being can only say "Pretty bird" so many times in one day, so I recommend buying an endless loop tape to continue the lessons while you're out. Incidentally, "pretty bird" is easier for most parrots to say than "hello," so you might be wise to start with that phrase and work up to the greeting.

Teach the bird one word or one phrase at a time. Once it has learned one phrase, it shouldn't take as long to teach it others. However, most people report a plateau period, after which the parrot pretty much stops learning new words. Not surprisingly, that plateau usually corresponds to the point when the human got tired of holding lessons, making tape recordings, and so on. If you want your parrot to go on learning, you must continue to teach it. A good talker should eventually be taught to repeat its name, your name, and your address; that way, if it's ever lost or stolen, it can identify itself to its finder or the police.

Parrots learn to talk to please their owners, so some people may be disappointed when their birds refuse to speak for visitors. To coax the parrot into speaking, you need to understand that it may be shy about attracting the attention of a stranger. A good way to get the bird talking is to move away from its cage and get involved with something else. Once you and your guest are busy with your own conversation, the parrot can satisfy itself that the guest is harmless and work up to surprising you with a sudden "Hello."

Also, remember that most wild parrots would be very reluctant to make noise when the jungle or savannah was deathly quiet. If you sit in silence waiting for the bird to say

A Scarlet Macaw riding its "bike." Parrots can be taught a number of tricks as long as patience and understanding are utilized by their owners.

something, it may never speak. But if you run some water, play some music on low volume, or get on with your own conversation, the parrot is much more likely to join in.

One more note about talking: it really isn't cute or funny to teach your parrot objectionable language. You'll soon tire of a bird that can't be enjoyed around sensitive friends and family, and the bird won't understand why it's being shut away from others when it was just trying to please you. Of course, any talking parrot, like any small child, can try to win attention by picking up words that they sense will elicit strong emotion. The best thing to do is to ignore the parrot, refusing to laugh or fuss or anything else that would encourage it to repeat the word. Make an extra effort to prevent the parrot from hearing the word from others, and after awhile it should forget how to

say it—or at least how to say it clearly enough that anyone but you will know what it's up to.

Besides talking, parrots can learn a variety of other tricks. If your bird is flighted, I suggest that the first lesson you teach it is to "come" on command. Choose a time when it seems eager to play and place it on top of its cage or perch. Step back and ask it to come in a firm, pleasant voice. When it flies to your shoulder, praise it and scratch its ears. Repeat the lesson often. After awhile, the parrot will learn to associate the word "come" with the action of flying to your shoulder, and it will fly to you on command. I don't promise that the trick will work if the bird ever escapes to the baffling and unfamiliar outdoors, but it gives you a chance.

Some people paper-train their parrots, a chore that's usually easier with a hand-reared bird. Choose a strange word that wouldn't come up in normal conversation, so that you won't unintentionally give the word when the parrot is perched on your new shirt. At first, simply wait until it looks like the parrot is about to go in an acceptable spot. Say the word, and praise the bird if it defecates at the same time. Repeat the lesson frequently, saying the word and then praising the bird any time it defecates over its paper. Over time, it will associate the magic word with the act of defecation, and you will be able to give the word first. Then you can forestall or eliminate accidents by taking it for a quick trip to its paper every 20 minutes or so and giving the command.

Other tricks are just for fun, but they serve a serious purpose. Pet parrots, especially the larger ones, can get lazy. By teaching tricks, you'll encourage your parrot to stretch its mind while exercising its body. You'll also give it a great way to attract the attention that pet parrots thrive on.

Start with tricks based on the parrot's natural behaviors. Most large parrots enjoy holding their food in a claw as they eat, so you can easily teach them to use a metal spoon. Attach a favorite minced fruit to a spoon with a thin coat of honey, and watch the parrot go! With time and practice, you can encourage it to actively pick up food from a bowl with a spoon.

Parrots are also drawn to bright, shiny objects. You

A Blue-headed Parrot (*Pionus menstruus*). When training your pet parrot, keep in mind that all birds are individuals with different abilities.

can play on this interest by setting up a metal bell at the top of a ladder. (Buy the toys from a pet dealer so you can make sure it's strong enough for your Macaw or Amazon.) If you place the parrot at the bottom of the ladder, chances are it will climb up as you give the command. Once at the top, it's likely to find the bell and start ringing. Great! Praise the bird, and offer it a treat or a head-scratching. Again, with time, you can encourage the bird to associate the words "climb up and ring the bell" with the trick so that it will perform on command with no hesitation.

Other favorite tricks include asking a parrot to place a clean penny in a bank, to join you in a gentle tug of war over a chain, or to ride a specially designed scooter or bicycle. Just keep in mind the basic principles for trick-training, and you'll be well on your way to teaching your bird a whole bag of tricks. To rehash, you'll find it easiest to teach tricks if you 1) choose tricks based on natural behaviors, like the desire to pick up shiny objects; 2) always use the same command words in connection with a given trick so that the bird can associate your words with the trick; and 3) give several short lessons that last under 20 minutes each time so you won't overload the parrot's short attention span.

Finally, you may have to do some training to overcome behavior problems. Most parrots will give a squawk of greeting when you come home, but you shouldn't have to put up with a parrot that shrieks morning, noon, and night. If the parrot is tame, chances are that it's squawking for attention. Are you giving it enough time out of its cage each day? Does it know any tricks or words that it can use to get your attention instead? If you're doing everything right and the parrot is still squawking all over you, place the bird in its cage and cover it each time it squawks to show it that loud noise isn't the way to win attention. Take it out and offer to play with it only when it has fallen silent. Never give a squawking parrot a treat or attention to "shut it up," or you'll be reinforcing the notion that making noise is a great way to win your attention.

It's especially disappointing when a tame parrot bites, but some do. Untame parrots bluff more often than not unless they feel cornered, but a tame parrot knows it has nothing to fear from you and may decide that biting is a good way to get its way. Whenever a parrot bites, say "No" in a loud voice and express your disappointment. However, don't make a habit of returning the bird to its cage as soon as it bites. Otherwise, it will think that biting is human talk for "I want to go in now." In addition to teaching it that biting is a no-no, you can minimize problems by being sensitive to your parrot's moods and attention span. If a tame parrot starts getting grouchy and tired, return it to its perch or cage for awhile. Give your parrot a balanced mixture of playtime and private time, and it should become a trustworthy sweetheart.

Occasionally, a one-time sweetie will turn grouchy. If your parrot is dancing around nervously, regurgitating food on you, and biting out of jealousy when your partner appears, it's probably in breeding condition—and, for the time being, it's showing its love for you by stating that it has chosen you for its mate. Exercise extra patience and firmness during this time if you can't or prefer not to breed the bird. If you would like to breed the bird—and if you have an exotic species you probably should to help produce parrots for the future to enjoy—then turn to the next chapter for a look at what's involved.

Headstudy of an Alexandrine Parrot. When training your parrot, remember that it can become bored and tired, and it may not have as long an attention span as its owner.

BREEDING PARROTS

Breeding parrots is an important hobby. If you breed domesticated species like Budgerigars and Cockatiels, you're helping to fill the demand for practical, loving parrots that can be kept by people who might otherwise not be able to have a pet. If you breed exotic species, you're helping to preserve these beautiful birds for the future. Besides, domestically raised parrots can be the sweetest, most talkative, and most trustworthy parrots of all simply because you can teach them from an early age that humans are their friends.

In the last twenty years, there have been some exciting changes in the world of parrot breeding. Time was when the only parrots that bred reliably in captivity were Cockatiels, Budgerigars, and Lovebirds—parrots that could tolerate relatively inferior diets and small cages. Other parrot breedings were few and far between, and some of the most interesting species were thought to be impossible to rear in captivity. Nowadays, many people are breeding Macaws, Amazons, Cockatoos, African Greys, and other parrots consistently and reliably. Most heartening, these breeders have usually been more than willing to share what they have learned about their birds so that others may emulate them. By consulting books and magazines for information about your species, you too can learn how to breed these fascinating birds.

Your first step is to make sure you have a true pair. Many species of parrots are monomorphic; that is, the males and females look alike. Although experienced breeders who have many individuals to work with can often guess the sex of each bird by subtle clues, beginners who guess usually guess

FACING PAGE:
A pair of Pacific Parrotlets. Before attempting to breed any pair of birds, be sure that both are in excellent health and physical condition.

wrong. Many a Max has gone on to lay eggs, and many a Josephine has ended up with her name shortened to Joe. If your parrot has never laid an egg and belongs to a monomorphic species, have it sexed before advertising for a female. You may just have to reword that ad.

Surgical sexing is the most reliable method for sexing birds. When performed by an experienced vet, it's almost always right and it permits the vet to see if the sexual organs are ripe for breeding. However, you may not want to have your parrot sexed because of the small risk of death or injury that is present with any surgical procedure. In that case, you may opt for a safer, if less certain, method such as pelvic sexing. This technique involves feeling between the pelvic bones of a sexually mature bird, preferably when it's perching. If the bones are spaced apart, the bird is probably a female. If they're close together, it's probably male.

Thankfully, some species of parrots offer more obvious clues. Adult male normal Cockatiels, for instance, have conspicuous yellow face patches that the females lack. Male Budgies in breeding condition usually have blue ceres (the skin around the nostrils), while females usually have pink or tan ceres. Some Australian Grass Parakeets can be distinguished when you see both sexes together, since the males generally sport brighter colors. Male Ringneck Parakeets develop striking black rings around their necks, although sometimes not until a year or more after they're sexually mature. Eclectus Parrots show a most striking sexual dimorphism that's the reverse of what's usually expected. The Eclectus female is the vivid red one, while the male is dressed in a quietly beautiful green.

If you would like to buy a breeding pair instead of a potential mate for your pet, be careful. You may be better off buying several young birds and waiting for them to become sexually mature so that you can pair them off yourself. A proven pair of breeding parrots represents an investment in time and money that has the potential to pay off in valuable youngsters for many years, so you need to ask why the breeder is willing to sell. It could be that the breeder has run out of room and must scale down operations, but it could also be that said proven pair has never done anything but lay infertile eggs

because it's actually made up of two females.

It's easy to get impatient, but don't encourage your parrots to start breeding too young. Hens in particular need to build up their systems before beginning on a breeding project. Otherwise, their bodies could steal vital nutrients from their bones and organs to form their eggs, placing their lives in danger. Besides, young parrots are usually too restless to make good parents. Parrots can live a long time, so you might as well err on the conservative side.

So how long must you wait before setting up parrots to breed? It depends on the species. Smaller birds like Lovebirds and Budgerigars will do fine if they're a year old, while you may have to wait as long as four to eight years to start breeding a large Macaw or Cockatoo. Again, I urge you to read whatever you can find on the species you plan to breed.

In years past, people feared that a pet parrot who had chosen a human "mate" was ruined for breeding. However, patient breeders have shown that pet parrots can be coaxed into accepting a more appropriate mate. In the long run, former pets often make better parents because they're confident around people and hence unperturbed about breeding in cap-

A pair of Blue and Gold Macaws. Since Macaws have such long lifespans, they take longer than most parrots to come into breeding condition. It may take up to eight years for a Macaw to become sexually mature.

tivity. However, they're also less afraid of biting humans who invade the breeding territory, so set up the flight pen so that you can check on the contents of the nest box and change the food and water dishes without placing your hands inside.

Feathers could fly if you try to plop two parrots together without a proper introduction, especially if one of the birds thinks it already has you for a mate. Start the birds off in the same room but in separate cages. Let them observe one another while you gradually reduce the amount of time you spend playing with your pet. At first the two birds may indulge in a lot of hissing, shrieking, or threat-displaying across the room, but after a few days or weeks they will calm down and start to notice that the other bird's harmless. At that point, they'll begin to demonstrate a more benign curiosity toward each other. Move the cages a little closer together. Soon the parrots will start pressing against the sides of their cages in an effort to play with one another. They may even attempt to pass special treats from one cage to the other. Great. They're ready to move into their breeding quarters.

A Rainbow Lory. A proper diet is essential to a successful breeding program, as extra nutrition is necessary for the production of healthy chicks.

A Sun Conure incubating an egg. Captive-bred Sun Conures are very much in demand in the parrot trade.

Most parrots are highly territorial. Unless you're breeding Lovebirds, Budgerigars, or Quaker Parakeets, you should plan on placing only one pair of parrots in a breeding pen. (The exceptions are colony nesting birds that often do better in an aviary containing several pairs.) Cockatiels and some small parrots will breed in commercially available cages, but you should plan on building a long flight cage for the other species. To keep the breeders in top condition, give them a flight that's long enough to let them fly around a little. Furnish it with sturdy perches, preferably natural ones, but leave out distracting toys. Don't bother planting in the parrot aviary, since the hookbill will make short work of any vegetation.

People have bred large parrots indoors, believe it or not. If you have a spare room that's secure and well-lit, you may be able to place the flight cage within. For best results, replace the lighting with full spectrum (not broad spectrum) fluorescent tubes. This form of lighting, which mimics the wavelengths of light produced by natural sunlight, may help the birds produce some of their own vitamin D and hence keep them in better shape.

If you can manage it, you may prefer to build your flight pen outdoors. Don't forget to include an enclosed portion which can be shut off from the elements when the weather

turns bad. When planning the flight pen, remember that it must keep predators and thieves out—and chewing birds inside. Also, check with your neighbors and investigate the local zoning laws to make sure it's legal to build an aviary where you live. Sometimes, laws aimed at restricting backyard chicken coops or pigeon lofts can be used to prohibit parrot flights.

Most parrots are cavity nesters, which means they would nest in hollow trees or in termite mounds in the wild. Hence, they don't build their nests, they find them. Many smaller parrots can use commercially available Budgie or Cockatiel nest boxes, depending on the size of the species.

You'll have more trouble locating nest boxes for the larger parrots. A wooden nest box large enough for a Macaw could seem painfully expensive—especially once the Macaws chewed a gaping hole in its side. Fortunately, many large parrots will accept a strong metal nest box that won't get chewed up in a few days. Where to get said nest box? Turn a clean metal outdoor garbage can on its side, and voila. Even a Macaw will have room to go to nest inside. However, metal is a good conductor of temperature, so the garbage can nest should be removed during extremes of hot or cold.

You should always give your parrots the best diet you can, but make a special effort when your birds are breeding. Once the babies are hatched, offer plenty of soaked and sprouted seed, sprinkled lightly with a vitamin and mineral supplement, in addition to the rest of the diet. You may want to hand-feed the parrots yourself in order to rear the best possible pets. If so, keep in mind that it's best to let the natural parents care for their chicks for the first ten days so that they can "infect" them with beneficial intestinal bacteria which will help them resist future illnesses. Besides, it's tedious to hand-rear a very young baby that needs feeding at half-hour intervals. Let the parents take care of this chore if they will.

You can make a very cozy brooder for the babies you hand-feed by using an old aquarium tank lined with soft towels that you will change every day. Get a screen lid to fit the tank when you're out of the room, to protect the babies from curious pets, kids, or visitors, and set up a heating pad near one end of the tank to keep the babies warm. For best results, be-

A pair of Turquoisine Parrots. Before placing two birds together in a breeding area, be sure they are properly introduced.

ginners at hand-feeding should obtain one of the commercially available mixes instead of trying to formulate their own.

As you can see, we've only discussed the bare outlines of what's involved in breeding your parrot. For best results, take advantage of those who have gone before you by joining a bird club, asking others what they've done, and reading the books and magazine articles on your species. All your work, worry, and research will pay off the moment a sweet-faced, half-feathered baby looks up to you and says, "Hello."

A WORLD OF PARROTS

There are well over 300 species of parrots distributed around the world. Let's take a look at some of the characteristics of the groups you're most likely to meet.

Lories and Lorikeets, the Brush-tongued Parrots, are small to medium-sized birds extravagantly decorated in all colors of the rainbow. Although they're more work to feed than most other parrots, experienced parrot owners enjoy them for their active natures and clownish personalities. Favorite Lories include the scarlet Red Lory (*Eos bornea*) and the gaudy Rainbow Lory (*Trichoglossus haematodus*), both of whom seem born to play. If you're buying an imported Lory to train as a pet, look at the eyes. Adults with orange or yellow eyes will be much more difficult to tame than the youngsters whose eyes are still dark.

Lories are messier than other parrots because of their diet, so you'll need to clean their cages and perches more frequently. If you line a Lory's cage with paper, you'll find yourself changing it several times a day. To save time and prevent odor, choose a deep-bottomed tray that can be filled with an absorbent litter like pine shavings or ground corncobs.

Cockatoos and their close relatives, the ever-popular Cockatiels, are a group of Australasian parrots with handsome crests, affectionate personalities, and a unique white powder down on their feathers. Hand-reared White Cockatoos have an incredible need for physical affection, petting, hugging, and snuggling. Don't acquire one of these birds if you can't play with them on a daily basis. A neglected Cockatoo may resort to uncontrollable screaming or restless feather picking, and both

FACING PAGE:
A pair of Eclectus Parrots; the male is the green bird and the female is the red. Captive Eclectus Parrots can make wonderful pets, but they should be encouraged to get regular exercise.

habits are very hard to break. The Umbrella Cockatoo (*Cacatua alba*) is a widely available species known for its striking looks and high intelligence.

More people keep Cockatiels (*Nymphicus hollandicus*) than any other kind of parrot except the Budgerigar. They're easy to care for, moderately priced and medium sized, and full of affection for their humans. In recent years, a whole galaxy of Cockatiel mutations has been developed by breeders. Favorites include the lovely yellow lutino and the richly spangled pearly.

The lovely Eclectus (*Eclectus roratus*) is the color-coded parrot with the red females and the green males. For many years, scientists thought that the two sexes belonged to different species! As you might expect with such a strongly dimorphic bird, the brilliant red female tends to be more aggressive than the male, but both birds can become affectionate pets that enjoy human handling. It's very difficult to distinguish between the four available subspecies, so beginning breeders should make every effort to get in touch with more experienced breeders who can help them pair up members of the same subspecies. Since pet Eclectus Parrots can run to fat, encourage yours to eat more vegetables and less oily seeds.

Australian parakeets are hardy ground-feeding birds of particular interest to hobby breeders. They're approximately the size of the Cockatiel, but they need long flights, rather than cages, for breeding. They're usually kept in pairs for breeding, although hand-reared specimens are occasionally available. Although beautiful and easy to feed, they may not be the best choice for a beginner. If kept outdoors, they often acquire worms from their frequent contact with the ground, so you need to consult with a vet about a regular de-worming schedule. The eight species of Rosellas tend to be so aggressive that pairs can't be kept in side-by-side flights or they'll spend all their time bickering. The lovely Scarlet-chested Parakeet (*Neophema splendida*) and Turquoisines (*N. pulchella*) are endangered species in the wild that have been saved from extinction by captive breeders. Both of these sexually dimorphic species are fairly easy to breed, and some breeders are now working on developing a variety of color mutations in these birds. The Bourke Parakeet (*N. bourkii*) has a rosy mutation that produces

a dramatic rose-pink plumage that's nothing short of breath-taking.

The Budgerigar (*Melopsittacus undulatus*), a small parakeet with a gentle nature and a chatty voice, is beyond a doubt the most popular pet parrot in the world. If they're tamed when they still have barring on their foreheads, they make sweet, affectionate pets that relish life with a human family. If kept in groups for breeding, they're happy to produce beautiful eggs and chicks. Budgerigars are highly recommended for beginners. Because of the many beautiful mutations that can be developed for show or sale, they also continue to challenge the experienced aviculturist.

The three subspecies of African Greys (*Psittacus erithacus*) are famous for their talking ability and, once tame, their need for attention. Before obtaining one of these gifted mimics, the beginner needs to be aware that untame Greys usually require a lot of time and patience to train. In the same way that a human baby might seem like a slow starter next to a baby

A lovely blue mutation of the Quaker Parakeet. Quakers are very good breeders, and for this reason are often used as foster parents for chicks of other breeds.

gorilla, these intelligent parrots demand a heavy initial investment in training time. As a result, hand-reared Greys are in
great demand and can cost four times or more what an import
does. They're worth it! Well-trained Greys can entertain you
with snatches of conversation, imitations of everything from
the family dog to the telephone, and demands (sometimes in
human tongue!) for head-scratchings and treats.

Taming an adult Grey, often referred to as a growler,
is no job for a beginner. To make sure that you're getting a
young bird, insist on a Grey with dark eyes. It's true that some
Greys' eyes lighten up before they're too old to tame, but an
inexperienced person is in no position to judge whether that's
the case with a particular bird. To ensure that you'll get the pet
you're dreaming of, be extra-picky when shopping for an African Grey.

The Senegal Parrot (*Poicephalus senegalus*) and
Meyer's Parrot (*P. meyeri*) are smaller African parrots who
aren't fussy about diet. Surprisingly, they often breed better in

Meyer's Parrot. Meyer's
Parrots are prone to
nervousness in large
areas; therefore, they do
not require as large a
breeding area as some
other species.

Blue and Gold Macaws are probably the most common Macaws kept in captivity. Therefore, those interested in this breed should not find them difficult to locate.

roomy cages than in aviaries, apparently because they get nervous in exposed areas. As with the African Greys, the demand for the intelligent hand-reared babies usually far exceeds the supply. If you must buy an import for a pet, get a young bird who still has dark eyes and rather dull feathers.

Lovebirds have a special place in the bird-keeping hobby. The Peach-faced Lovebird (*Agapornis roseicollis*) is a beautiful pocket parrot that comes in a variety of lovely color mutations. The popular species breed well in colony aviaries. Unlike most other parrots, they need willow twigs, palm fronds, or other nesting material, since they will actually build a snug little nest of their own inside the box. Hand-reared Lovebirds make incredibly affectionate pets that demand petting and attention on a daily basis. A busy person might prefer keeping a pair of Lovebirds together for their beauty; in that situation, the birds will be happy to play with each other all day and, therefore, won't become fully tame. If you want to tame a Lovebird for a pet, look for a youngster that still has some black on its beak.

The elegant Asian parakeets are excellent talkers with slim bodies and long tails. The Indian Ringneck Parakeet (*Psitta-*

cula krameri borealis) is the most widely available. In addition to the ability to speak up to 250 words, these birds have a lutino (yellow) mutation that's absolutely breathtaking. African Ringnecks (*P.k. krameri*), Alexandrines (*P. eupatria*), and some other species are also sometimes available. The hand-reared babies of all these species are highly recommended as pets.

Moving on to the wonderful South and Central American parrots, we arrive first at the various interesting species of Macaws. These long-tailed birds with bare face patches are the colorful giants of the parrot family. These birds can have a wicked sense of humor, and it's easy for a beginner to be intimidated by their powerful beaks and confident manner. For that reason, beginners should probably avoid untame specimens.

Hand-fed Macaws are affectionate, snuggly parrots who are much more likely to talk than wild-caught specimens. Hand-fed Blue and Gold Macaws (*Ara ararauna*) are the gentle giants most likely to be available to a beginner without a lot of contacts in the bird hobby. Hyacinth Macaws (*Anodorhynchus hyacinthinus*) and Scarlet Macaws (*Ara macao*) are also popular, but since they have been recently listed as endangered species, they really belong in breeding flights, not living rooms.

Conures, small cousins of the Macaws, are interesting mid-sized parrots that are coming into their own as pets and breeders' birds. Although these graceful parrots can be noisy, they make affectionate pets if tamed young. Hand-fed Conures are even better, since the noise they make is often human chatter! The Sun Conure (*Aratinga solstitialis*), one of the most beautiful birds in the world, is a popular bird that's regularly hand-fed for the pet market. The other species such as the Peach-front Conure (*A. aurea*) and the Nanday Conure (*Nandaya nenday*) possess less show good looks, but they're equally intelligent and can make excellent pets.

Quaker Parakeets (*Myiopsitta monachus*) are highly adaptable parrots with some unusual characteristics. They breed in colonies, building enormous communal nests in the tops of trees. Although they originated in South America, small colonies formed by escaped birds have established themselves in New York, Chicago, and probably some other areas. Because they could present competition to native birds (or farmers!),

A Grey-cheeked Parakeet. When purchasing one of these birds, it is recommended that you look for a young bird, as older Grey-cheeks may become set in their ways.

some states forbid you to keep these birds. Check with your wildlife department. If you're permitted to keep Quakers and you're serious about breeding medium-sized parrots, strongly consider keeping pairs of these reliable little breeders to care for abandoned eggs or babies from the nests of touchier species.

Parrotlets are charming little birds small enough to breed in cages. They are easy to sex by eye, since males have blue wing markings that the females lack. The most common species is the Pacific Parrotlet (*Forpus coelestis*), a cute little bird with a quiet, almost tuneful, song.

Grey-Cheeked Parakeets (*Brotogeris pyrrhopterus*) are inexpensive little parrots that do well in Cockatiel cages. Sweet-

natured, hand-fed babies become available on a regular basis since South American collectors remove chicks from the nest for some degree of taming and human care before sending them on to export. However, they make nippy pets indeed if you wait until they're grown up to start taming them.

Two other groups of mid-sized Latin Americans are the Caiques and the Pionus. Caiques are smallish, white-breasted parrots that have bred in cages. They like to burrow under covers or into a dark nest box to sleep, so provide a roost box even if you keep just one as a pet. Pionus Parrots are gentle, stocky parrots who should be bred in flight pens. Hand-fed babies from both groups are conveniently packaged pets with the playfulness and intelligence of a much large parrot.

Amazons are the stocky green birds that everyone thinks of first when you say the word "parrot." Renowned talkers with outgoing personalities, the Amazons make fiercely loyal pets that can withstand a certain amount of separation from their owners. As they mature, they tend to develop definite opinions about who and what they like. Older birds can be bad about deciding that only one person or one sex is acceptable, making it necessary to transform them from family pets into members of a breeding pair. However, many people are willing to put up with a certain amount of bossiness from their Amazons in exchange for sharing their lives with these special birds.

Some Amazons have a natural odor. It's perfectly normal, so don't worry about it, as long as the bird and its cage are kept clean. All Amazons can get lazy and go to fat, so encourage them to play often and to eat an assortment of fruits and vegetables. Imported and domestic hand-fed babies can both make great pets, but domestic Amazons should be first choice, since they don't have to go through the stress of quarantine. Start working with an Amazon from an early age, and watch it amaze you with its quick grasp of mimicry and trick-training.

The following books by T.F.H. Publications are available at pet shops everywhere.

PARROTS OF THE WORLD
By Joseph M. Forshaw (PS-753)
This book covers every species and subspecies of parrot in the world, including those recently extinct. Information is presented on the distribution, status, habitats, and general habits. Almost 500 species and subspecies are illustrated in full color on large color plates.
This remarkable and beautiful book, valued almost as much for its sheer good looks as for its highly valuable information, is a delight to bird-lovers and book-lovers alike.

SUGGESTED READINGS

PARROTS AND RELATED BIRDS
By Henry J. Bates and Robert L. Busenbark (H-912)
This is the "bible" for parrot lovers. It has more color photographs and more information on parrots than any other single book on the subject. Written primarily for the owner of more than one parrot or parrot-like bird, this book is a necessary reference work for libraries, pet shops, and airport officials who must identify imported birds.

TAMING AND TRAINING PARROTS
By Dr. E. Mulawka (H-1019)
This book deals effectively with Dr. Mulawka's proven methods of successful parrot training. In this volume, which is heavily illustrated with both color and black-and-white photographs, the author imparts his techniques for cultivating a pet parrot's innate abilities to learn.

Index